GILPIN COUNTY PUBLIC LIBRARY

DATE DUE

OUTSTANDING AFRICAN AMERICANS

GREAT AFRICAN AMERICANS IN

THE OLYMPICS

SHAUN HUNTER

Crabtree Publishing Company

Dedication

This series is dedicated to the African-American men and women who followed their dreams. With courage, faith, and hard work, they overcame obstacles in their lives and went on to excel in their fields. They set standards as some of the best Olympic athletes in the world. They brought innovation to film, jazz, and the arts, and the world is richer for their touch. They became leaders, and through their example encouraged hope and self-reliance. *Outstanding African Americans* is both an acknowledgment of and a tribute to these people.

Project Manager
Lauri Seidlitz

Production Manager
Amanda Howard

Editor
Virginia Mainprize

Copy Editor
Janice Parker

Design
Warren Clark

Layout
Chris Bowerman

Photograph Credits
Cover: Devers photo (Bettmann: Niedringhaus), Joyner photo (Bettmann: Ake), Foreman photo (Bettmann: Hershorn); **AFP/Corbis-Bettmann:** pages 6 (Anja Niedringhaus), 9 (Eric Feferberg), 26 (Romeo Gacad); **Canapress Photo Service:** page 41 (Paul Chiasson); *The Calgary Herald:* page 44 (Bruce Stotesbury); **Globe Photos:** pages 4, 8, 55 (Barry Bland), 10 (Andrea Renault), 16 (Angelo Frontoni), 18 (Bob Noble), 25, 46 (Chuck Muhlstock), 27 (Stephen Trupp), 28 (Adam Scull), 32, 40 (John Barrett), 33 (Tom Rodriguez), 35 (Fionnbar Callanan), 37 (John Evans), 38 (Walter Weissman), 45 (Tony Guzewicz), 21, 23, 42; **Reuters/Corbis-Bettmann:** pages 5 (Charles Platiau), 7, 15, 36 (Gary Hershorn), 58 (David Thulis); **UPI/Corbis-Bettmann:** pages 22 (David Ake), 24 (David Boe), 29 (Ray Lipski), 39 (Ron Kuntz), 43 (Blake Sell), 11, 12, 13, 14, 34, 49, 52, 61; **Urban Archives, Temple University, Philadelphia, Pennsylvania:** page 19; **U.S. Olympic Committee:** pages 17, 20, 30, 31.

Every reasonable effort has been made to trace ownership and to obtain permission to reprint copyright material. The publishers would be pleased to have any errors or omissions brought to their attention so that they may be corrected in subsequent printings.

Published by
Crabtree Publishing Company

350 Fifth Avenue,
Suite 3308
New York, NY
U.S.A. 10018

360 York Road, R.R. 4
Niagara-on-the-Lake
Ontario, Canada
L0S 1J0

73 Lime Walk
Headington
Oxford OX3 7AD
United Kingdom

Cataloging-in-Publication Data

Hunter, Shaun, 1961–
    Great African Americans in the Olympics / Shaun Hunter.
        p.   cm. — (Outstanding African Americans)
    Includes index.
    Summary: Presents biographies of thirteen African Americans, including Edwin Moses, George Foreman, Debi Thomas, and Florence Griffith Joyner, who have won medals at the Olympics.
        ISBN 0-86505-823-7 (pbk.). — ISBN 0-86505-809-1 (lib. bdg.)
        1. Afro-American athletes—Biography—Juvenile literature. 2. Olympics—Juvenile literature. [1. Athletes. 2. Afro-Americans—Biography. 3. Olympics.] I. Title. II. Series.
GV697.A1H86   1997
769′.092′2—dc20
[B]
                                                        96-46148
                                                            CIP
                                                             AC

Contents

For other great African Americans in Olympics, see the book

GREAT AFRICAN AMERICANS IN SPORTS
Jackie Joyner-Kersee • Carl Lewis • Jesse Owens •
Wilma Rudolph...and others!

Gail Devers

Personality Profile

Career: Track-and-field athlete.

Born: November 19, 1966, in Seattle, Washington, to Larry and Alabe Devers.

Education: B.A., University of California at Los Angeles (UCLA), 1988.

Awards: Pan American Games gold medal, 1987; World Championship silver medal, 1991; Olympic gold medal, 1992; two World Championship gold medals, 1993; World Championship gold medal, 1995; two Olympic gold medals, 1996.

Growing Up

When they were children in San Diego, California, Gail Devers and her older brother used to race each other in the backyard. Her brother would make fun of Gail every time he beat her. "One day," Gail remembers, "I decided I wasn't going to lose anymore, and I started practicing on my own." The next time they raced, she won, and her brother never raced her again. Gail's brother began organizing races between his sister and the neighborhood children. Gail always beat them easily. As she remembers, "From then on, running and track were all that mattered."

Born in 1966 to a Baptist minister and an elementary school teacher's aid, Gail grew up in what she describes as a typical American family. She has fond memories of happy family times, picnicking, playing touch football, singing, and Bible studies. As a young girl, she wanted to be a teacher. She borrowed her mother's school books and taught the neighborhood children to read when they came to play.

Gail won a gold medal in 1992 by running the women's 100-meter in 10.82 seconds.

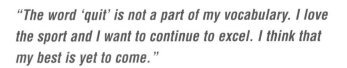

"The word 'quit' is not a part of my vocabulary. I love the sport and I want to continue to excel. I think that my best is yet to come."

Developing Skills

Gail began running track seriously in high school, starting out as a long distance runner. Even though she did not receive much coaching, she did well at the California high school track championships. She placed first in the 100-meter dash and 100-meter hurdles, and third in the long jump competition.

The summer before she started college at the University of California (UCLA) in 1984, Gail went to the Los Angeles Coliseum to see the Olympic trials. There she asked the sprinter Valerie Brisco to point out the women's track coach at UCLA, Bob Kersee. At that time, he was coaching some of the top women sprinters, such as Valerie Brisco, Florence Griffith Joyner, and Jackie Joyner. Soon after meeting Gail, Bob told her to watch as much of the Los Angeles Olympics as possible. This would help her to start thinking of herself as a top international runner instead of as a high school champion.

Gail won the 100-meter hurdles at the 1995 World Championships in Stockholm, Sweden.

That autumn, Gail began classes at UCLA and started training with Bob Kersee. Bob is a coach who expects all his athletes to give their best. In 1984, he could already see Gail making the Olympic team in 1988 and bringing home gold medals in 1992. Bob set out to help Gail develop her running skills and change her attitude toward sprinting. He thought she needed to learn how to be more aggressive during her races. By her senior year of university, Gail had learned a lot from Bob. She set a new American record, running the 100-meter race in just 10.86 seconds.

Gail has competed against the best athletes in the world, including Michelle Freeman of Jamaica.

Accomplishments

1987 Won first place in the 100-meter race at the Pan American Games.

1988 Graduated with B.A. in Sociology from UCLA.

1991 Overcame a three-year battle with Graves' Disease. Set U.S. record in the 100-meter hurdles.

1992 Won an Olympic gold medal in the 100-meter race in Barcelona, Spain.

1993 Became the first woman in forty-five years to win a gold medal in both the 100-meter sprint and 100-meter hurdle events in an international competition.

1995 Won World Championship gold medal in the 100-meter hurdles in Sweden.

1996 Won two Olympic gold medals in the 100-meter sprint and the 4x100-meter relay in Atlanta, Georgia.

Overcoming Obstacles

Gail made the U.S. Olympic team in 1988. A month before the Games, she began feeling ill. She had trouble breathing and suffered from migraine headaches. Her doctors said she had asthma. Gail went to the Olympic Games in Seoul, South Korea, anyway. She ran poorly, not even making the finals. For the next two years, Gail's health got worse. She had fits of shaking, had trouble remembering things, and started to lose her sight. Her doctors did not know what was wrong. Gail finally saw a specialist in 1990. Her mysterious illness turned out to be Graves' Disease.

In 1996, Gail won Olympic gold in the 100-meter final in Atlanta, Georgia.

With Graves' Disease, a gland at the base of the neck produces too much of a hormone called thyroid. The eyes begin to bulge, legs swell, and body weight goes up and down rapidly. Gail's thyroid gland was enlarged and contained a lump the size of a child's fist.

People with Graves' Disease can be treated with drugs. These drugs, however, are on the banned list for Olympic athletes. Not wanting to ruin her drug-free record, Gail chose radiation treatment. She was not prepared for the harsh side effects of radiation. She lost hair and blood. Her feet became so swollen and blistered that she could no longer stand. Her parents moved in with Gail to take care of her. In March 1991, a doctor told her she was just days away from having both her feet amputated. Gail remembers, "Deep down inside, I was scared to death that I was finished as an athlete."

Gail immediately changed her treatment and began an amazing return to health. In April 1991, for the first time in two years, she walked once around the UCLA track, without her shoes and in a great deal of pain. By May, she was back at the track, running hurdles. In June, she won a 100-meter hurdle race. Later that year, she received a silver medal at the World Championships in Tokyo, Japan.

In 1992, she won her first Olympic gold medal in Barcelona, Spain, for the 100-meter sprint. Four years later, at the Atlanta Olympics, Gail ran against the best athletes in the world, including her teammate Gwen Torrence and the Jamaican sprinter Merlene Ottey. In an exciting photo-finish race, Gail leaned into the finish line and won her second Olympic gold medal for the 100-meter event. A few days later, she won a third gold medal as part of the U.S. 4x100-meter relay team.

With the help of her coach, Bob Kersee, Gail overcame a crippling disease to win Olympic gold.

Special Interests

- Gail has always enjoyed teaching young children. She dreams of one day opening her own daycare center.
- Gail loves to read. She especially loves long novels, which she races through in two or three days.
- Gail crochets, does crossword puzzles, and has a collection of stuffed animal monkeys.

George Foreman

Personality Profile

Career: Boxer.

Born: January 10, 1949, in Marshall, Texas, to J. D. and Nancy Foreman.

Family: Married five times. Has nine children.

Awards: Olympic gold medal, 1968; world heavyweight title, 1973; inducted into U.S. Olympic Hall of Fame, 1990; world heavyweight champion, 1994.

Growing Up

In the book about his life, George Foreman wrote, "Almost from the time I was born, anger and hunger shaped my youth." George grew up in a tough neighborhood in Houston, Texas. His mother worked hard to feed her seven children. By the time George was a teenager, he was bigger than most other teens and hot tempered. His friends were a crowd of petty criminals. George learned to solve his problems with his fists. Back then, George has said, "I thought a hero was a guy who came back from prison."

In 1965, when George was sixteen, his sister told him about the Job Corps. This government program educated and gave job skills to young people from low-income backgrounds. It changed George's life. He remembers an ad in which the football star Jim Brown described the Job Corps as a place to "get a second chance." Realizing he needed such a chance, George signed up and moved to Oregon.

Although George was a good student and worker, he was still a bully. He remembers, "Looking at me sideways or any which way...earned you a knuckle sandwich with relish." One evening, he and others were listening to a Cassius Clay fight on the radio. One fellow said to George, "You're always picking on people....Why don't you become a boxer?" George accepted the challenge. He moved to another Job Corps center in California with a boxing program.

"Overnight I became a poster boy for the Job Corps: I'd gone from being a junior high dropout to a young man who now devoured books; from unemployable teenager to skilled factory worker; from thug to humanitarian."

Developing Skills

"None of [my victories] felt as good as when I was poor and had just won that gold medal, when I wore it so long I had to have the ribbon restitched."

George quickly took to boxing. Instead of beating up people, he got rid of his anger and showed his strength in the boxing ring. After just two years and eighteen amateur fights, George qualified for the U.S. Olympic team and headed for Mexico City in 1968. He won a gold medal, but his victory was not cheered by all Americans.

At the Mexico Olympics, two African-American athletes, Tommie Smith and John Carlos, raised their fists in the black power salute when they were given their medals. They wanted to show the world their protest against racism in America. When George received his gold medal, he was so pleased that he proudly waved a small U.S. flag. This angered many African Americans who thought George should have shown support for Smith and Carlos.

After his Olympic win, George left amateur boxing and turned professional. At six feet, three inches tall and 220 pounds, he was a frightening opponent. He was unbeaten in forty fights in a row, winning many in the first two rounds. As he told *Sports Illustrated* magazine, "My opponents didn't worry about losing to me. They worried about getting hurt."

In 1973, George prepared to fight Joe Frazier, the man who had beaten the boxing legend Muhammad Ali. George made headlines by beating Joe in a savage match. He managed to knock Joe down six times. People were amazed. They had thought Joe Frazier was unbeatable.

A year later, George fought Muhammad Ali himself in Zaire, Africa, in front of 62,000 boxing fans. Muhammad was the crowd's favorite. He let George fight hard for the first six rounds until George was tired. Then Muhammad knocked him down in the eighth round, winning the match. It was a terrible loss for George, and it took him ten years to pull his life and his boxing career back together.

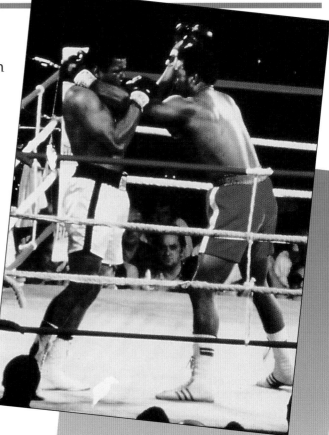

George fought boxing legend Muhammad Ali in Zaire, Africa.

Accomplishments

1968 Won an Olympic gold medal in heavyweight boxing.	**1987** Returned to the boxing ring.
1973 Won the world heavyweight title.	**1994** Won World Boxing Organization heavyweight title.
1977 Retired from boxing. Founded the Church of the Lord Jesus Christ in Houston, Texas.	**1995** Co-wrote his autobiography, *By George*.

Overcoming Obstacles

After his loss in Zaire, George returned to his ranch in Marshall, Texas. He thought money could help him forget his defeat. He bought expensive cars and exotic pets and spent $400,000 in three months. He was filled with frustration and often became violent. Looking back, George admits his life was out of control. His surprising loss to Jimmy Young in Puerto Rico in 1974 was the final straw. George was so shaken by his defeat that he fell apart mentally and was taken to a hospital.

During this time, George claimed to have a religious vision that set him on a new path. He quit boxing and decided to devote his life to religion. He returned to Houston to preach on street corners and in local churches. He started his own church in a run-down building and devoted himself to preaching. Later, he founded the George Foreman Youth and Community Center to keep troubled kids off the streets.

After not boxing for ten years, George decided in the late 1980s to get back into the ring. His youth center desperately needed money, and he had a large family to support. George longed to be a champion again.

During a difficult time in his life, George turned to religion and began preaching throughout Texas.

George had numerous obstacles to overcome. The media laughed at him, calling him an old, overweight boxer. He had to lose over fifty pounds and get into shape. He attached a heavy punching bag to the back of his truck and ran behind it for ten miles every day, punching the bag. He also had to get over his own doubts about his comeback. To do this, he developed a sense of humor. As he laughed at himself, he also became popular with the public.

George weighing in before his fight against Evander Holyfield in 1991.

In 1991, George lost a fight to Evander Holyfield after twelve rounds. In 1994, against great odds and to the surprise of many, George won back the world heavyweight title. In his match against Michael Moorer, a boxer half George's age, George wore the same red boxing trunks that he had worn when he fought Muhammad Ali in Africa twenty years earlier. When the judges declared George the winner in the tenth round, he dropped to his knees in prayer.

Special Interests

- George has three sons named George.
- At the time he began spending all his money, George owned a lion, a tiger, and a $21,000 German shepherd.
- George loves fast food. Before his comeback, he weighed about 315 pounds.

Rafer Johnson

Personality Profile

Career: Track-and-field athlete.

Born: August 18, 1935, in Hillsboro, Texas, to Lewis and Elma Johnson.

Family: Has two children, Jenny and Josh.

Education: University of California at Los Angeles (UCLA), 1957.

Awards: Pan American Games gold medal, 1955; Olympic silver medal, 1956; *Sports Illustrated* sportsman of the year, 1958; Olympic gold medal, 1960; James E. Sullivan Award for best amateur athlete in the United States, 1960; inducted into U.S. Olympic Hall of Fame, 1983.

Growing Up

Rafer experienced poverty and racial discrimination throughout his childhood. When he was a year and a half, his family moved to a black ghetto in Dallas, Texas. Rafer's memories of those years are unhappy ones. Looking back, he once said, "I don't care if I ever see Texas again."

In 1945, when he was ten, Rafer's family moved outside of Kingsburg, about twenty miles south of Fresno in central California. While his father worked for the railroad, Rafer and his family lived in a railway boxcar near a canning factory. An old curtain down the middle of the car divided it into two rooms for the family of seven. Later, the Johnsons moved into Kingsburg. Although at first they felt unwelcome because they were black, they decided to stay in the town.

As a boy, Rafer loved playing baseball and had a reputation for hitting the ball so hard he regularly broke the bat. In high school, he was one of the top athletes in basketball, football, baseball, and track-and-field.

In his junior year of high school, Rafer's track-and-field coach invited him to a nearby town to see Bob Mathias compete at a local meet. Mathias had won two Olympic gold medals for the decathlon in 1948 and 1952. Rafer remembers, "On the way back it struck me. I could have beaten most of the guys in the meet. That's when I decided to be a decathlon man."

Developing Skills

O ne month after seeing Bob Mathias, Rafer won the California Junior Amateur Athletic Union (AAU) decathlon championship. One year later, as a high school senior, he finished third at the National AAU Championships in Atlantic City.

Rafer's athletic skill, along with long hours of practice, launched his career as a decathlete. The decathlon is perhaps the most difficult of all track-and-field sports. It is made up of ten events held over two days. The first day, athletes compete in the 100-meter dash, long jump, shot put, high jump, and the 400-meter race. The second day, they finish with the 110-meter hurdles, discus throw, pole vault, javelin throw, and 1500-meter run. Athletes receive points according to a special set of score tables. The event is exhausting, and people view the winner of the decathlon as one of the best athletes in the world.

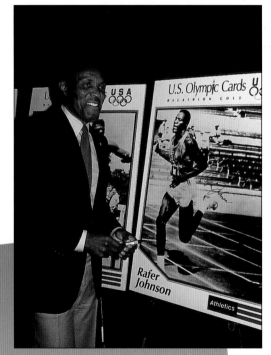

Rafer was honored many times for his athletic accomplishments.

As a champion decathlete, Rafer received two dozen scholarship offers from colleges across the country. He chose to stay close to home, and in 1955, he started at UCLA. As a physical education major, he kept a straight B average all through college. In his senior year, his fellow students elected him president of the student body. He also served as campus leader for the national movement Youth for Christ. On the track, he became friends with Yang Chuan-kwang, a student from Taiwan. Rafer helped him train as a decathlete, even though he knew Yang would offer him tough competition.

During his UCLA years, Rafer was an excellent athlete. In 1955, he won a gold medal at the Pan American Games in Mexico City. Shortly after, at a meet in his hometown, he broke Bob Mathias's world decathlon record. He was only nineteen years old. In 1956, Rafer was a member of the U.S. team at the Olympics in Melbourne, Australia. A long-time decathlete from New Jersey, Milton Campbell, won the gold medal that year, and Rafer placed second.

As a student at UCLA, Rafer combined his studies with training for the 1960 Olympics.

Accomplishments

1955 Won the gold medal for the decathlon at the Pan American Games in Mexico City.

1956 Won the silver medal for the decathlon at the Olympics in Melbourne, Australia.

1957 Graduated from UCLA with a degree in physical education.

1958 Named sportsman of the year by *Sports Illustrated* magazine.

1960 Won the gold medal for the decathlon at the Olympic Games in Rome, Italy. Given the James E. Sullivan Award and named one of the nation's ten outstanding young men of the year by the U.S. Junior Chamber of Commerce. Signed a contract with Twentieth Century Fox.

1980s Served as national head coach of the Special Olympics.

Overcoming Obstacles

Injuries caused Rafer problems all through his career as an athlete. When he was twelve years old, a conveyor belt at a peach canning factory trapped and tore his left foot. Years later, Rafer still had trouble wearing spiked track-and-field shoes because of the old injury. During the 1956 Olympics in Melbourne, Rafer was suffering from painful injuries to his knee and from pulled stomach muscles. In 1959, one year before the Rome Olympics, he was in a serious car crash. He could not train for almost a year. He made a remarkable recovery, and at the Games, he won the gold medal and set a new Olympic record.

Rafer became known as one of the best athletes in the world when he won the Olympic decathlon in 1960.

Rafer always pushed himself to the limit. His experience at the Rome Olympics is a good example of the pressures Rafer had to deal with in the decathlon. The first day of competition lasted until 11 P.M. At the halfway point, Johnson edged ahead of his friend Yang by a few points. The second day began poorly for Rafer when he knocked over the first hurdle in the 110-meter race. He regained points in the pole vault with his best performance ever.

The final test was in the last race, the exhausting 1500-meter run. If Yang could beat Rafer by ten seconds, Yang would win the gold medal for Taiwan. At 9:15 P.M., after twelve hours of competition, the race started. Yang won the race but did not have enough points to win the decathlon, so Rafer took the gold. At the end of the race, the two college friends fell against each other for support. The crowd chanted, "Give them both the gold!"

Because Rafer was both a fine athlete and a model citizen, he was asked to carry the American flag in the opening parade at the Rome Olympics. He was the first African American to be given this honor. More than twenty years later, he lit the Olympic torch at the 1984 Los Angeles Games.

In recent years, Rafer has worked hard for people with mental and physical disabilities through the Special Olympics. He believes that being an athlete gives all people, whatever their race, class, or disability, the opportunity to be equals.

Rafer with his son, Josh.

Special Interests

- Two months after he won his Olympic gold medal in Rome, Rafer signed a contract with the movie studio Twentieth Century Fox and appeared in three action-adventure films. He has also been a television sportscaster.
- Rafer has worked for many years with mentally and physically handicapped people. He has been involved in the Special Olympics and served as its national head coach during the 1980s.
- In his spare time, Rafer enjoys skiing, playing the guitar, and taking photographs.

Florence Griffith Joyner

Personality Profile

Career: Track-and-field athlete.

Born: December 21, 1959, in Los Angeles, California, to Robert and Florence Griffith.

Family: Married Al Joyner, 1987. Has one child, Mary Ruth.

Education: University of California at Los Angeles (UCLA).

Awards: National Collegiate Athletic Association (NCAA) championship, 1982; Olympic silver medal, 1984; three Olympic gold medals and one silver medal, 1988; James E. Sullivan Award for best amateur athlete in the United States; named athlete of the year by the Associated Press and the Soviet news agency Tass, 1988; given the Jesse Owens Award for outstanding track-and-field athlete of the year.

Growing Up

Being an athlete has been a part of Florence Griffith Joyner's life ever since she was a little girl. In 1966, when she was seven, she started running in races at the local community center. She loved to run. She quickly realized she was fast—faster than most of the boys her age. Part of her earliest training came from chasing jack rabbits in the desert near her father's home.

Florence was the seventh of eleven children. When Florence was six years old, her mother and father separated. Her mother moved her large family to a housing project in the Watts district of Los Angeles, California, where she raised them with a firm hand. The children did not watch television. They took their studies seriously and had a family meeting every Wednesday to read the Bible and discuss their problems. Florence's mother worked hard to support her children. She taught them to be strong and independent.

"My mother had no choice but to be independent and I think I got that from her—being able to stand on my own two feet. She taught us all that nothing is going to be handed to you—you have to make things happen."

As a girl, Florence had many interests besides sports. She loved fashion and sewed clothes for her dolls. She also enjoyed cosmetics and hairstyling and spent hours braiding her friends' and neighbors' hair. She liked to stand out in a crowd. When she was in kindergarten, she braided her hair with one braid sticking up straight. Once, she wrapped her pet boa constrictor around her neck and walked through a local shopping mall.

Developing Skills

n high school, Florence won prizes for sprinting and long jump. Before she graduated in 1978, she had broken several high school track-and-field records. Florence had no plans to pursue these sports. She just thought of them as a way to keep fit. She went to California State University at Northridge to study business. At the end of her first year, she had to drop out because she did not have enough money for her fees. Florence found a job as a bank teller.

While she was still at California State, an assistant track coach named Bob Kersee had noticed Florence's talent as a sprinter. When she had to leave college, Bob helped her get financial aid to return. Then, he started training Florence for the 200-meter sprinting event. In 1980, when Bob moved to Los Angeles to coach the UCLA women's track-and-field team, Florence followed. She had decided to be a runner and knew Bob was the coach for her. She worked hard to get a place on the U.S. track-and-field team going to the 1980 Olympics in Moscow, but she finished fourth in the 200-meter Olympic trials. As it turned out, no American athletes competed in Moscow. The United States did not send any teams to the 1980 Olympics to protest the Soviet Union's invasion of Afghanistan.

With a love for fashion, Florence designed many of her own running outfits.

Florence's training paid off in 1982 when she won the National Collegiate Athletic Association (NCAA) championship in the 200-meter dash. She tried out again for the Olympic team, and this time she made it. At the 1984 Olympic Games in Los Angeles, California, Florence lined up in the starting block, her long fingernails painted red, white, and blue—with one gold nail for good luck. Many first-time Olympic athletes would have been thrilled with Florence's silver medal in the 200-meter race. But Florence was disappointed with her second-place finish. She got a job in a bank during the day, styled hair at night, and cut back on her training.

Florence was never happy with being second best. She was determined to triumph at the 1988 Olympics.

In 1986, the next Olympics was just two years away. Bob Kersee and Florence's boyfriend, Al Joyner, a triple-jump gold medalist, encouraged Florence to give track-and-field another try. She began training hard. This time, she wanted to be the best in the world, not second best.

Accomplishments

1982 Won the National Collegiate Athletic Association championship for the 200-meter race.

1984 Won a silver medal in the 200-meter race at the Olympic Games in Los Angeles.

1988 Won three Olympic gold medals and one silver medal in Seoul, South Korea.

1995 Inducted into the U.S. Track-and-Field Hall of Fame.

Overcoming Obstacles

Many things stood in Florence's way of winning a gold medal at the 1988 Olympics in Seoul, South Korea. She had just two short years to get back into top form. How could she work full time and train? How could she afford to train without working full time? At first, she worked all day in the bank and trained until late at night. Later, she found a job in a company that helped Olympic athletes. Florence worked four hours a day and spent the rest of the day and evening training.

At Seoul, South Korea, Florence won three Olympic gold medals and one silver.

Florence and Al were married in 1987, and soon Al became her coach. Each day, he worked long hours with Florence on the track and in the gym. He encouraged her to believe she could win the gold. In the trials for the U.S. Olympic team, Florence beat the world record in the 100-meter sprint. At the Olympic Games in Seoul, she continued to hold the spotlight. In four days of races, she broke four records and won gold medals in the 100- and 200-meter races and the 4x100-meter relay. She also won one silver in the 4x400-meter relay. This was the most medals ever won by an American female track athlete.

Florence, or Flo-Jo as everyone called her, also dazzled the crowds with her brightly colored running suits and her long, decorated fingernails. She made herself the center of the world's attention and fulfilled her Olympic dream. Soon, her face began to appear on magazine covers all over the world. However, rumors began that she had used steroid drugs to help her performance. Drug tests have never proved this.

Florence is honored as one of ten great sports legends.

In 1989, Florence retired at the top of her career. Since then, she has kept busy designing sport clothes, putting out an exercise video, and creating a line of Flo-Jo nail products. She has also helped set up recreation centers for low-income, young people.

Special Interests

- Florence co-chairs the President's Council on Physical Fitness and Sports. She is the first woman to hold this position.
- Florence created a fitness video, "The Flo-Jo Workout: Mind, Body and Spirit."
- Besides track-and-field, Florence has many interests and talents. She enjoys acting, writing, painting, designing clothes, and modeling.

Sugar Ray Leonard

Personality Profile

Career: Boxer.

Born: May 17, 1956, in Wilmington, North Carolina, to Cicero and Getha Leonard.

Family: Married Juanita Wilkinson, 1980, (divorced, 1990); married Bernadette Robi. Has two children, Ray, Jr., and Jarrel.

Awards: National Golden Gloves titles, 1973-74; amateur light-welterweight champion, 1974-75; Pan American Games gold medal, 1975; Olympic gold medal, 1976; world welterweight champion, 1979; world junior middleweight champion, 1981; world middleweight champion, 1987; world light-heavyweight champion, 1988; world super-middleweight champion, 1989; named boxer of the decade, 1990.

Growing Up

When he was fourteen years old, Ray Leonard went along with his best friend to the local community center in Baltimore, Maryland. A quiet, skinny boy, Ray joined the center's boxing program. His coach had made a boxing ring with strips of tape on a basketball court. After a few months, Ray had learned so much that his coach told him he could be a boxing champion.

Ray Charles Leonard was the fifth child in a family of seven children. His mother was a music fan and had named him after the famous rhythm and blues singer Ray Charles. As a young boy, Ray sang in the church choir. As a teenager, he dedicated himself to boxing.

Ray's parents worked hard to provide for their large family. Often, Ray and his brothers and sisters could not afford the money to go on school field trips. In grade school, Ray was a loner and an outsider. When he started to box, he found something he could do well. He had the sense of balance, quick movements, and instincts of a boxer. He copied the moves he had seen Muhammad Ali and other great boxers use in their fights. When the assistant coach of the U.S. Olympic boxing team saw Ray fight, he told Ray's coach, "That kid of yours is sweeter than sugar." From then on, Ray was known as Sugar Ray, a name that reminded people of the 1950s boxing legend, Sugar Ray Robinson.

"We were poor.... But I always knew I could get out. I could sing. I was a terrific gymnast.... And I found boxing, but it was just a means to an end, a way to make people respect who I was...."

Developing Skills

When Sugar Ray was just sixteen, he began his boxing career by winning one of the greatest amateur boxing awards, the Golden Gloves championship. He was allowed to join the American Athletic Union (AAU) national team, even though he was not yet seventeen, the age required to join the AAU. The AAU chairman thought Sugar Ray was the best amateur lightweight boxer in the United States and wanted him on the 1972 Olympic team. At the Olympic trials, Sugar Ray was beaten by Greg Whaley. Even today, most people think the referee made a mistake. This was Sugar Ray's first loss since he had begun boxing. He would have to wait until 1976 to go to the Olympics.

Sugar Ray in the 1976 Olympics.

For the next four years, getting to the Montréal Olympics was Sugar Ray's main goal. He turned down many offers to become a professional boxer. Day after day, he trained, in spite of painful, swollen hands. For hours, he studied the styles and movements of the world-famous boxers he would meet in Montréal.

The media liked Sugar Ray and called him a sure medal winner. Photographers liked his smile, and reporters were attracted by his easy-going personality. Many people thought he put the sparkle back into welterweight boxing. In Montréal, Canada, he won all his matches. In the final fight, he beat Cuban boxer Andres Aldama. It was Sugar Ray's 150th amateur fight and his 145th win. After his victory, Sugar Ray announced that he would retire from boxing: "My decision is final. My journey has ended. My dream is fulfilled."

Sugar Ray after winning Olympic gold in 1976.

Accomplishments

1976 Won Olympic gold medal in the light-welterweight class in Montréal, Canada.

1976 Became a professional boxer and formed his own company, "Sugar Ray Leonard Inc."

1979, 1981 Named fighter of the year by *The Ring* magazine.

1980 Set world record for the most money earned in a single fight ($9.5 million) against Roberto Duran.

1981 Named ABC's athlete of the year.

1981 Won about $10 million in a fight against Thomas Hearns, the highest amount ever earned by a professional boxer in a fight.

1987 Broke his own 1981 record by collecting $11 million in his fight against Marvin Hagler.

1991 Retired from boxing as the first boxer to win titles in five weight classes, from welterweight to super-middleweight.

Overcoming Obstacles

"When you saw me in the ring, you really saw three people. You saw me. You saw my mother's grace and her fire. You also saw my father's determination to overcome terrific odds."

In 1973, while he was still training for the 1976 Olympics, Sugar Ray's high school sweetheart, Juanita Wilkinson, told him she was pregnant. They decided to wait until after the 1976 Olympics to get married. For three years, Sugar Ray devoted all his time to training and to Juanita and their baby boy. Unlike his friends at school, he did not have time for fun. Often, he thought about giving up boxing. With the support of his family and his coaches, Sugar Ray stuck to his goal.

Sugar Ray was named Boxer of the Decade in 1990.

At the Montréal Olympics, Sugar Ray fought the match with badly injured hands. He was in constant pain, and his opponent fought well and hard. But when the final bell rang and Sugar Ray was declared the winner, he knew it had been worth the pain and all the years of hard work.

After the Olympics, Ray planned to quit boxing and go to college. He also hoped to earn money for his family by endorsing products. Not only did Sugar Ray want to support Juanita and Ray, Jr., but his parents also needed his help. Shortly after the Olympics, his father fell ill with spinal meningitis, and his mother suffered a heart attack.

32

Sugar Ray's plans did not work out as he had hoped. He returned from the Olympics to be shocked by newspaper headlines about a lawsuit against him. While Sugar Ray had been training for the Olympics, Juanita was short of money and had applied for public assistance. Officials thought that Sugar Ray had refused to support his family, and they started a lawsuit against him, even though he planned to marry Juanita and look after his family. Because of the bad publicity, no company wanted Sugar Ray to endorse their products.

Sugar Ray Leonard with his second wife, Bernadette.

Changing his mind about leaving boxing for good, Sugar Ray became a professional boxer. Muhammad Ali had warned him about boxing promoters who would take most of his money. Sugar Ray decided to control his career and set up his own company, Sugar Ray Leonard Inc.

Sugar Ray's boxing career took off quickly. Soon, he was earning millions of dollars for his fights. After fifteen years of professional boxing, he retired in 1991.

Special Interests

- In 1984, Sugar Ray became a television boxing commentator for the HBO television network.
- Sugar Ray is beginning a new career in acting. Recently, he finished working on a pilot series for television and a made-for-television movie.
- Sugar Ray continues to stay physically fit. He works out at the gym three hours every day and plays golf regularly.

Edwin Moses

Personality Profile

Career: Track-and-field athlete and bobsled racer.

Born: August 31, 1955, in Dayton, Ohio, to Irving and Gladys Moses.

Family: Married Myrella Bordt in 1982.

Education: B.Sc., Morehouse College, 1976.

Awards: Olympic gold medal, 1976; James E. Sullivan Award for best amateur athlete in the United States, 1983; Olympic gold medal, 1984; member of the U.S. Olympic Hall of Fame, 1985; Olympic bronze medal, 1988; member of the National Track-and-Field Hall of Fame, 1994.

Growing Up

Edwin Moses began his track-and-field career late. His parents were both school teachers, and Edwin grew up in a family where books, art, and music were very important. In high school, he ran track for fun after class. Because he was small for his age, no one encouraged him to pursue a career in sports.

An excellent student, Edwin won a scholarship to Morehouse College, a black men's school in Atlanta, Georgia, and studied physics. Sports were not stressed at Morehouse, and the college had no space for track-and-field training. Edwin trained on his own, running for exercise and as a break from his studies.

In the middle of his final year at college, Edwin started to take track seriously. His height had spurted to six feet, two inches, and his speed and power as a runner had improved. With his long legs and strong body, he seemed to float over the hurdles. Edwin set his sights on competing in the 400-meter hurdles at the 1976 Olympic Games in Montréal, Canada. Before the Olympics, Edwin ran the hurdle races at the Florida Relays. Although he did not win any of his races, he finished with impressive times, especially in the 400-meter hurdles. One coach remarked, watching Edwin run, "Compared to Ed, everyone else looked like roosters with their tails on fire."

"I think my main motivation is that I really do love the sport of track-and-field…. I gave up a career in engineering to stay in track-and-field; I've sacrificed a lot for the sport."

Developing Skills

Edwin finished first in his heat at the 1988 Olympics but did not win gold in the finals.

Good 400-meter hurdlers need special skills to run a quarter mile and clear the ten, three-foot hurdles in their path. They need speed, size, stride, and strength. Edwin had all of these. Part of Edwin's success lay in his ability to take thirteen steps between each hurdle for the whole race. Other hurdlers could not keep up this pace and dropped to fourteen or fifteen steps near the end of a race.

Before the 1976 Olympic trials, Edwin had competed in only two track meets. At one of these, Edwin's glasses fogged up in the rain, and he fell and lost. However, at the Olympic trials, he set an American record in his race.

At the Montréal Olympics, Edwin set a new world record and won a gold medal. He looked forward to earning a second gold medal at the next Olympic Games in Moscow in 1980. However, the United States decided not to send any teams to the games to protest the Soviet invasion of Afghanistan. Edwin lost his chance to win back-to-back gold medals. He had to wait eight long years until the 1984 Los Angeles Olympics before claiming his second gold medal.

In the meantime, Edwin improved his running time. In 1977, he lost for the last time in his career. From then on, it was one win after the other for the next nine years. During this long winning streak, Edwin broke his own record several times. From 1977 to 1986, he won 122 races in a row. At the 1984 Olympic Games, he easily won his second gold medal.

At the 1988 Olympics in Seoul, South Korea, the young American athlete Andre Phillips outran Edwin in the 400-meter hurdles to win the gold medal. In his victory speech, Andre praised Edwin as a role model for all track-and-field athletes. "Most of the credit has to go to Edwin Moses because he was my motivation, my incentive, and my idol."

A star on the track, Edwin was also a leader off the track, helping amateur athletes. Before 1988, athletes who turned professional and were paid were not allowed to compete in the Olympics and other important meets. Many amateur athletes had to turn professional to earn enough money to support themselves. Edwin worked to get the rules changed so that amateurs could get paid.

Edwin was an inspiration to many young athletes.

Accomplishments

1976 Set an American record in the 400-meter hurdles during the Olympic trials. Won a gold medal at the Olympic Games in Montréal.

1980 Won his forty-third straight victory in Milan and broke his own world record.

1984 Recited the Athletes' Oath at the opening ceremonies of the Los Angeles Olympics. Won his second Olympic gold medal. Chosen as one of the three American representatives to the International Amateur Athletic Foundation (IAAF).

1988 Won a bronze medal at the Olympic Games in Seoul, South Korea.

1989 Appointed chairperson of the U.S. Olympic Committee's substance abuse committee.

1990 Joined the U.S. bobsled team.

Overcoming Obstacles

In 1985, Edwin suffered a blow to his reputation. He was accused of trying to hire a prostitute who turned out to be an undercover policewoman. The news shocked the athletic community and the public. At his trial, the jury found Edwin not guilty. In spite of the verdict, Edwin's commercial sponsors backed away and refused to consider him for endorsement deals. Edwin lost a $1 million contract to endorse a popular soft-drink.

To help restore his public image, Edwin continued training and entering competitions. He also focused on community service. He gave 10,000 tickets to low-income children to attend a track meet in Los Angeles. He also worked for the cerebral palsy fundraising drive in 1986. Soon, he regained his reputation as one of the most respected athletes in the world.

Edwin at the Olympic Legends Awards in 1996.

In 1990, a new opportunity presented itself to Edwin. At age thirty-five, he left hurdling and joined the U.S. Olympic bobsled team. In his first international race, his team won in the four-man bobsled competition in West Germany and came third in the two-man race. Within his first year of bobsledding, he was ready to become one of the best brakemen in the world. He was a quick learner and a fine team player. However, Edwin decided to leave the bobsled team before the 1992 Winter Olympics, wanting to spend more time on track training.

Silver medalist Danny Harris, gold medalist Edwin Moses, and bronze medalist Harold Schmid stand at attention during a 1994 medal ceremony.

Special Interests

- For a long time, Edwin has been against drug use in sports. He served on a U.S. Olympic committee that developed a new drug-testing plan for athletes.
- Edwin likes scuba diving and wind-surfing. He drives a car with license plates reading OLYMPYN.
- Edwin is a licensed pilot and an aerospace engineer.

Debi Thomas

Personality Profile

Career: Figure skater.

Born: March 25, 1967, in Poughkeepsie, New York, to McKinley and Janice Thomas.

Family: Married Brian Vanden Hogen, 1988, (divorced).

Education: Stanford University, 1991; Northwestern University.

Awards: National figure skating title, 1986; world figure skating title, 1986; Olympic bronze medal, 1988; World Championship bronze medal, 1988.

Growing Up

When Debi Thomas was four years old, she went to an Ice Follies show with her mother. She was so thrilled by the stunts of Mr. Frick, the "King of Trick Skating," that she begged her mother for skating lessons. At age five, Debi enrolled in a skating class for little girls.

When Debi was ten, she began training as a competitive skater at a club near her home in San Jose, California. She loved skating, but at first her coach, Alex McGowan, did not think she had a special talent. "I never thought she'd be a world champion," he admitted later. But Debi trained hard, learning to skate exact, perfectly shaped figures. That year, she won her first competition. Two years later, Debi mastered the triple jump. This spectacular jump is extremely difficult, and even the Olympic skater Dorothy Hamill had skated only double jumps when she won the gold medal. Debi won a silver medal at the national finals when she was twelve, the first sign that she might become a champion.

To give herself more time to train, Debi did not go to school in the eighth grade and did her studies by correspondence. Despite all her practice, she won only fourth place in the regional finals and missed her chance to compete for the junior world figure skating championships. From then on, Debi and her mother decided that skating would take second place to her education.

"I had ridiculously large dreams, and half the time they came true."

Developing Skills

Debi returned to school and devoted the next four years to her studies and to improving her skating skills. Even though she spent a lot of her time at the skating rink, she was an excellent student. Debi learned early on that skating was "too unpredictable" a career to depend on all her life. She planned to be a doctor, specializing in sports medicine. By the time she finished high school, she had been accepted into three of the country's best universities, Harvard, Princeton, and Stanford.

Two years before going to university, Debi began skating again in competitions. She became well known for her spectacular jumps and her bold skating routines. In two years, from 1983 to 1985, she moved from thirteenth to second place in the U.S. figure skating finals. She also ranked fifth in the world. In 1986, her first year at college, she won the U.S. national championship. That same year, she won the world championship, the first African-American woman to do so.

Deciding to try for the 1988 Olympics, Debi quit college for a year and began full-time training. She decided to really work on the artistic side of skating. She asked the great ballet dancer Mikhail Baryshnikov for help. He coached her in her dance pieces as she prepared for the Olympic Games in Calgary, Canada.

In Calgary, all eyes were turned on Debi and the East German skater Katarina Witt who had won the world title from Debi in 1987. Unfortunately, their rivalry had become bitter and personal. Adding to the problem, both women had chosen to skate to the same piece of music for the final part of their programs. Although Debi skated well, she accepted the bronze that evening while Katarina won the gold. After another bronze medal at the World Championships in 1988, just one month after the Olympics, Debi retired from competitive skating.

Debi was the U.S. National Figure Skating Champion in 1986 and 1988.

Accomplishments

1986 First African-American woman to win a world championship in singles figure skating.

1988 Won a bronze medal at the Calgary Winter Olympics and in the World Figure Skating Championship in Budapest, Hungary.

1991 Earned her engineering degree from Stanford University in California. Debi was the first female athlete in thirty years to balance full-time university studies with athletic competition.

I t takes lots of money and long hours to become a championship figure skater. Debi and all her family had to work hard to launch her skating career. Her mother, father, and grandparents all chipped in to pay for her lessons and coaching. When she began to skate, Debi often wore second-hand skates that were so tight that they hurt her feet. Sometimes, she herself repaired her broken skates with glue. To save money, she learned to sew her own costumes. During the summers, Debi stopped taking lessons so her mother could save up to pay the bills.

Debi's coach, Alex McGowan, gives her advice before the 1988 Olympics.

Determined to keep up with her studies, Debi worked hard at high school. She trained at the skating club six hours a day, six days a week. For four years, her mother drove 150 miles a day, taking Debi to school, then driving her to the rink for practice, and picking her up after a long day.

Few skaters can go to college and keep practicing at the same time. Debi did both, but sometimes it was too much. Debi's coach was worried that her studies would interfere with her skating. In 1986, her first year of college, Debi was doing too much and became depressed. She gained fifteen pounds and tore up her application to the national championships. After a vacation and rest, she decided to enter the nationals, but she had only five weeks to train. Performing an incredible five triple jumps, Debi won first prize. For the 1987 national championships, she had just as little time to practice. She pushed herself so hard that she pulled muscles in both her legs. When she performed her program, she was in pain and lost her title.

Still trying to give time to both her studies and her skating, Debi arrived at the 1988 Calgary Olympics exhausted. She planned to begin her program with two triple jumps. However, after her first triple, she landed on both feet. This was a small error, but Debi was so discouraged that she made two more mistakes in her routine. As she later said, "My heart wasn't in it after the first...jump."

Bitterly disappointed, Debi retired from amateur skating. But she had always believed that her education came first. In 1991, she graduated from Stanford and later began her medical studies at Northwestern University. As she said about herself, "You can't look at skating and feel that it is the only accomplishment in your life. It's just not enough."

Debi showed great determination by practicing skating and going to college at the same time.

Special Interests

- Debi continued to pursue other interests while attending medical school. She wrote a pilot for a weekly television show and did sports commentary for a television station in Chicago.
- Debi dreams of starting a training center where young people will be able to develop their non-athletic careers alongside their athletic pursuits.

Evelyn Ashford

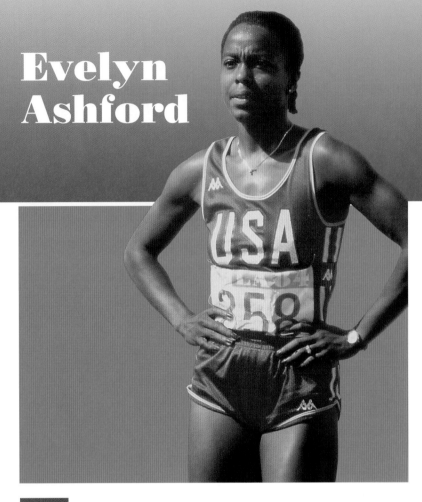

Evelyn Ashford was a late starter as a track-and-field athlete. In high school near Sacramento, California, Evelyn's math teacher noticed how fast she could run and arranged races between her and some of the boys on the track team. Evelyn easily beat them all. She was asked to join the boys' track squad, and by her senior year, she was co-captain of the team.

In 1975, Evelyn won an athletic scholarship to the University of California at Los Angeles (UCLA), one of the first offered to women. Her coach, Pat Connolly, remembers timing Evelyn's 100-meter dash on the first day of practice at UCLA. Pat could not believe her eyes. Right away, she knew Evelyn was good enough for the Olympics. Pat began training Evelyn, building up her speed and strength. She also taught her to believe in herself as a sprinter.

At the 1976 Olympics in Montréal, Canada, Evelyn placed fifth in the 100-meter dash. She began to see herself as a world-class sprinter. She went on to win race after race in the 100- and 200-meter events. By 1980, she was ready to compete in the Moscow Olympics. The U.S. decision not to send its teams to the games ended her hopes. It also put an end to her career for a while. Evelyn left track for a year. She wanted to think about her future and recover from the leg muscles she had torn during her races and training.

In 1981, she returned to the track, ready to win a gold medal in the 1984 Los Angeles Olympics. At the Los Angeles Games, Evelyn had two goals. She achieved the first, winning two Olympic gold medals, one in the 100-meter race and the other in the 4x100-meter relay. Her second goal was to beat her rival, sprinter Marlies Göhr. But this had to wait. Because the Soviet Union did not send its teams to the 1984 Olympics, Marlies did not run in the games. However, when Evelyn and Marlies did meet later that summer in Switzerland, Evelyn beat Marlies and set a new world record in the 100-meter race.

Personality Profile

Career: Track-and-field athlete.

Born: April 15, 1957, in Shreveport, Louisiana, to Samuel and Vietta Ashford.

Education: University of California at Los Angeles (UCLA).

Awards: World Cup champion, 1979; two Olympic gold medals, 1984; Vitalis Award for excellence in track-and-field, 1987; one Olympic gold medal and one silver medal, 1988; Olympic gold medal, 1992.

After having achieved her two goals—winning an Olympic gold medal and beating Marlies—Evelyn continued to train and race. She also became a sports commentator for the cable television program "World Class Woman." In 1988, Evelyn prepared for her third Olympic Games in Seoul, South Korea. She came second in the 100-meter race after her American teammate, Florence Griffith Joyner. In the 4x100-meter relay, she ran the anchor position for her team. Evelyn and her teammates won the gold medal.

In 1992, at the age of thirty-five, Evelyn competed in her fourth and final Olympics in Barcelona, Spain. As the oldest runner in the sprinting events, she won her fourth gold medal for the 4x100-meter relay. After a sixteen-year athletic career, Evelyn retired from running. She is now a successful business person and mother.

Accomplishments

1976-1992 Competed in four Olympic Games and won five Olympic medals.

1977, 1984 Named athlete of the year by *Track & Field News*.

1984 Became first woman to run the 100-meter sprint in under eleven seconds, setting an Olympic record.

1989 Awarded the Flo Hyman Trophy for supporting women's advancement in sports.

1992 Won an Olympic gold medal in the 4x100-meter relay in Barcelona, Spain.

Alice Coachman

A lice Coachman got her start as a high jumper early in life. When the neighborhood boys challenged her to jumping contests in a nearby field, Alice always won. Like many African Americans in the 1920s and 1930s, Alice did not have the same training opportunities as white children. She practiced jumping on the dirt roads and fields in and around Albany, Georgia. Only whites could train at track-and-field clubs.

Alice's parents were worried about her interest in sports. They thought that she was behaving too much like a boy. Alice remembers, "It was a rough time in my life. It was a time when it wasn't fashionable for women to become athletes and my life was wrapped up in sports. I was good at three things: running, jumping, and fighting." Alice's fifth grade teacher saw her student's talent and helped her get into athletics.

Like many African Americans in the 1920s and 1930s, Alice did not have the same training opportunities as white children.

In high school, Alice made the track team. She showed such talent that she was invited to go to Tuskegee Institute High School. At sixteen, even before she attended her first class at Tuskegee, she competed in a national championship meet for her new school. While she studied dressmaking at Tuskegee, she trained hard and won many competitions. By the time she was twenty-three, Alice had won four national track-and-field championships in sprinting and high jumping events. She was also an excellent basketball player, helping her team win three women's basketball titles.

Personality Profile

Career: Track-and-field athlete.

Born: November 9, 1923, in Albany, Georgia.

Education: B.A., Albany State College, 1949.

Awards: Twenty-five Amateur Athletic Union (AAU) track-and-field titles; Olympic gold medal, 1948.

World War II prevented Alice from competing in any world track-and-field events. Although they are usually held every four years, the Olympic Games were cancelled in 1940 and 1944. Alice made the team for the 1948 London Olympics. Although her back was sore and she was worried about being homesick, she decided to go. When she arrived in London, England, after a long boat trip, she was surprised to see her picture everywhere. The world was waiting to see her compete. Alice faced tough competition in the high jump at the Olympics. But with her first jump in the finals, she set a new Olympic record by jumping five feet six inches. She became the first black woman from any country to win an Olympic gold medal.

As a young girl, Alice had dreamed of becoming famous. In 1948, at the London Olympics, her dreams came true. King George VI awarded Alice an Olympic gold medal. When she arrived home, she was introduced to President Harry Truman and attended a victory party given by jazz musician Count Basie. In Georgia, she received a 175-mile motorcade from Atlanta to Albany and was cheered by both black and white fans. At the official welcome at the Albany Municipal Auditorium, however, she was greeted by a white-only audience and was not allowed to speak.

After she retired from running, Alice continued to inspire young African-American athletes. When she signed a contract with a famous soft drink company, she became the first African-American woman to be hired to endorse a product. Later, she established the Alice Coachman Track-and-Field Foundation to help young athletes. In 1996, she promoted the Olympics in Atlanta. Now in her seventies, she is still encouraging African-American athletes. Her advice to them is: "Don't let your dreams go away. Fight hard and have the guts to complete them."

Accomplishments

1948 First black woman to win an Olympic gold medal in any sport. First African-American woman to receive an international endorsement contract.

1936-1948 National high jump champion for twelve straight years.

1975 Elected to the National Track-and-Field Hall of Fame.

Jim Hines

I n junior high school in Oakland, California, Jim Hines was a keen basketball player. One day, the school track-and-field coach spotted Jim running and thought he would make a great sprinter. He asked Jim to try out for the track team. At the beginning of ninth grade, Jim ran the 100-yard dash in 10.6 seconds. In high school, he continued to improve his speed. By his senior year, he matched the great sprinter Jesse Owens's high school record, running 100 yards in just 9.4 seconds.

Jim was offered scholarships by several colleges. He chose Texas Southern in Houston because it had one of the best track-and-field teams in the country and one of the top coaches.

While he was still at college, Jim ran against Charlie Green, the American sprinter who was breaking world records. They became rivals for the position of fastest sprinter in the world. Both Charlie and Jim made the American Olympic track-and-field team. They would be part of the team representing the United States at the 1968 Olympic Games in Mexico City. One sports writer called them "the fastest four-legged sprinter ever sent to the Olympics."

Shortly before the 1968 Olympics, Jim almost quit track. He could not afford to support his wife and one-year-old son. The Miami Dolphins football team had offered him a good contract, which would solve his financial problems. After much thought, Jim decided "to go for the goal I had set for myself in college." The goal was an Olympic gold medal.

Personality Profile

Career: Track-and-field athlete.

Born: 1946, in Dumas, Arkansas.

Education: Texas Southern University.

Awards: Amateur Athletic Union (AAU) title, 1967; Olympic gold medal, 1968.

In Mexico City, the 100-meter finalists lined up at the starting blocks in front of 60,000 spectators. All the runners were black—the first time this had happened in Olympic history. Jim remembers, "As soon as I hit the tape I knew it had to be the greatest race of my life." Jim set a new world record of 9.95 seconds and won the gold medal. Jim's Olympic time remained the world record for nearly fifteen years, until Carl Lewis beat it at the 1988 Olympics.

Days after his victory, Jim signed a contract with the Miami Dolphins. However, Jim's football career was short. Because he had not played college football, he did not have the skills needed to do well at the sport. He had trouble catching the ball and spent most of his time on the bench. Some players on the team were jealous of his high salary. Soon, he was dropped from the team. Jim tried out for other football teams and continued to run professional races. After a while, both football and racing opportunities dried up completely. Eight years after winning an Olympic gold medal, Jim had no job. No one remembered him as the fastest runner in the world.

Jim found a new career as an agent for athletes. He also helped abused and neglected children through a special housing project. Jim spent a lot of time with these street kids, trying to give them a sense of hope for their future. A priest, who worked with Jim, said that "He's a great morale-booster. The message Jim gets across to them is that they can succeed as long as they try."

Accomplishments

1967 Equaled the world record in the 100-meter dash, running the race in ten seconds flat.

1968 Set new world record in the 100-meter dash (9.95 seconds) which remained unbroken until 1988. Signed a contract with the Miami Dolphins football club.

Michael Johnson

U ntil he got to university, Michael was a better student than he was an athlete. His parents encouraged their five children to work hard and do well at school. Michael played football in junior high school, but he found the sport too rough. At Skyline High School in Dallas, Texas, Michael decided to give track-and-field a try. The coach, who remembers Michael then as "just another skinny kid," let him run at the school track.

Michael practiced every day, but he did not catch the coach's attention. When Michael's time began to improve, some of his teammates suggested to the coach that Michael should run in the next meet. The coach did not even remember him but put him on the mile relay team. Michael competed in many track events but never stood out as a star.

Michael's trademark is his gold lamé running shoes, which he has specially made for him.

When Michael applied to Baylor University in Waco, Texas, the coach there noticed him and decided to use him to fill out some of his relay teams. He offered Michael an athletic scholarship, even though he thought Michael "looked more like a...scholar than a track athlete."

Personality Profile

Career: Track-and-field athlete.

Born: September 13, 1967, in Dallas, Texas, to Paul and Ruby Johnson.

Education: Baylor University.

Awards: World Champion, World Athletics Championship, 1991 and 1993; Olympic gold medal, 1992; U.S. Olympic Committee Athlete of the Year, 1993; Jesse Owens Award, 1994; U.S.A. Track-and-Field Athlete of the Year, 1993-94; double World Champion, 1995; two Olympic gold medals, 1996.

Michael began training for the 1988 Olympics in Seoul, South Korea, but because of a problem with his leg, he never made it to the Games. The next year, he missed most of the outdoor track season because of pulled leg muscles. In 1990, however, his career took off when he started a forty-seven-race winning streak in his top two events, the 200- and 400-meters. These two races require very different skills. To run the 200-meter sprint, athletes need speed. For the 400-meter race, they also need incredible strength. Michael is one of the few runners in the world who has both.

At the 1992 Olympics in Barcelona, Spain, Michael had a good chance of winning the gold medal in the 200-meter race. Six weeks earlier at the Olympic trials, he had beat his teammates and Olympic gold champions, Carl Lewis and Michael Marsh. Food poisoning just before the games, however, caused him to miss qualifying, and he did not make the team.

Disappointed, Michael set a new goal: to be the fastest male sprinter in the world in both the 200- and 400-meter events. In 1995, Michael was well on his way to achieving his goal, winning double world championships in Sweden.

During the 1996 Olympic Games in Atlanta, Georgia, Michael amazed the world. He broke the Olympic record in the 400-meters and the world record in the 200-meters. In front of a roaring crowd in Atlanta, he ran the 200-meter race 0.36 seconds faster than his fastest competitor, Frank Fredericks of Namibia. Michael was the first male runner to win both races at the Olympics.

Many people think of Jesse Owens when they think of Michael Johnson and his accomplishments. Never one to boast about his record-breaking career, Michael says, "Jesse Owens is my idol, but please don't compare me to him. I don't face the same pressures he did."

Accomplishments

1990, 1991, 1994 Ranked first in the world in the 200- and 400-meter races by *Track and Field News*.

1993 Ranked first in the world for the 400-meter event.

1994 Received the Jesse Owens Award for outstanding track-and-field athlete of the year.

1990-96 Undefeated in the 400-meter event, winning forty-four races in a row.

1996 First man to win gold medals in both the 200- and 400-meter events at the same Olympic Games.

Gwen Torrence

W hen she was just seven months old, Gwen Torrence was walking months before most children. By the time she was a year old, she was talking. Gwen's mother remembers the last of her five children having something special. "The first time I laid eyes on Gwen, she had this look in her eyes. I didn't tell anybody, but I said to myself, this baby's going places."

"Whatever we did as kids, I was the fastest."

Gwen lived in the East Lake Meadows housing project near Atlanta, Georgia. When Gwen was in elementary school, her family suffered two blows. Their father died, and an accident paralyzed the oldest brother, Charles. Gwen's mother worked as a housekeeper to support the family, and the children pulled together, helping one another through difficult times.

Gwen always knew she could run fast. She was the fastest runner on the local softball team. In high school, Gwen outran the fastest player on the football team. But her physical education teacher, Ray Bonner, had to work hard to convince her to try running the 220-yard dash. Gwen finally joined the track team. Shy and skinny, she refused to wear shorts and sneakers during practices because she was ashamed of her long, thin legs. She preferred to train alone after school. Soon, she turned out to be a top high school sprinter.

Universities from across the United States offered Gwen athletic scholarships. Her teacher, Mr. Bonner, remembers that "she didn't care. She said she wanted to be a hair stylist, to work at Rich's or Macy's department store." Mr. Bonner finally convinced Gwen to enroll at the University of Georgia. She began a remedial program, but within a year, she made the dean's list for good grades. She also ran for the university team, winning four important track-and-field events in 1986 and 1988.

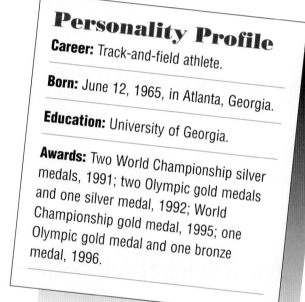

Personality Profile

Career: Track-and-field athlete.

Born: June 12, 1965, in Atlanta, Georgia.

Education: University of Georgia.

Awards: Two World Championship silver medals, 1991; two Olympic gold medals and one silver medal, 1992; World Championship gold medal, 1995; one Olympic gold medal and one bronze medal, 1996.

In 1988, Gwen began training for the 1992 Olympics. She qualified for the U.S. track-and-field team in four events. At the games in Barcelona, Spain, Gwen won a gold medal for the 200-meter race, another for the 4x100-meter relay, and a silver medal for the 4x400 relay. She won more medals than any track-and-field athlete at the Games.

Gwen became known for her outspoken comments off the track. In Barcelona, she placed fourth in a close 100-meter event. After the race, she accused three of the other runners of using steroid drugs to improve their speed. She had no proof and later apologized. However, the year before she had been beaten by a German runner who later tested positive for drug use.

At the 1996 Olympics, held in her hometown of Atlanta, the public had high hopes for Gwen. Suffering from exhaustion and an injured leg, she ran only the 100-meters and the 4x100 relay, not the 200-meters. In an extremely close final in the 100-meter race, Gwen finished third. Her comments after that race showed a wiser and calmer person. "I was happy to be in the finals. I had accepted victory or defeat before it even happened.... I'm so much more relaxed now. I'm not going to let track ruin [me] the way it has in the past."

Accomplishments

1986 Made the dean's list at the University of Georgia.

1991 Ranked first in the United States in the 100- and 200-meter races.

1992 Youngest finalist in her events at the Olympics in Barcelona, Spain; represented the U.S. team in four track-and-field events.

1995 Named top American female athlete overall by *Track and Field News*. Voted athlete of the year by the International Track Federation.

1996 Olympic bronze medal in the 100-meter sprint at Atlanta, Georgia.

Wyomia Tyus

I n the 1940s and 1950s, many children in Griffin, Georgia, had to work in the cotton fields to help support their families. Wyomia and her three older brothers were different. Their father would not allow his children to work. As Wyomia remembers, "Our responsibility was to go to school and get an education." Every day, Wyomia rode the bus for an hour to school because the neighborhood school was for whites only.

Wyomia's father also encouraged his daughter to get involved in competitive sports. This was unusual at a time when most people thought competition was "unladylike." As Wyomia said, "To be African American in Georgia at that time, there was nothing to do. And if you were poor, you could do even less. Track gave me opportunities."

When Wyomia was just fifteen, Ed Temple, the track coach from Tennessee State University (TSU), saw her compete. He invited her to his summer track-and-field camp. Wyomia's family could not afford to send her, but her high school friends raised the money for her to go. The extra training paid off quickly. When she was just seventeen, Wyomia set the American record for her age group at the Amateur Athletic Union (AAU) championships.

Wyomia decided to attend TSU to continue training with Ed Temple. At that time, only male athletes got college scholarships. Wyomia had to work to pay for her education and training. At TSU, she became a member of the Tigerbelles, a top-ranking track team to which the great sprinter Wilma Rudolph had belonged. Wyomia qualified for the Olympic team heading for the Tokyo Games in 1964. Her teammate, Edith McGuire, was favored to win the gold medal in the 100-meter race. In a surprise victory, Wyomia won the top honors. Four years later, she continued her winning streak at the Olympic Games in Mexico City where she won two gold medals for the 100-meter race and the 4x100 relay. She also set a new world record.

Personality Profile

Career: Track-and-field athlete.

Born: August 29, 1945, in Griffin, Georgia, to Willie and Maria Tyus.

Education: Tennessee State University, 1968.

Awards: Amateur Athletic Union (AAU) title, 1964; Olympic gold medal, 1964; Pan American Games gold medal, 1967; two Olympic gold medals, 1968; member of the National Track-and-Field Hall of Fame, 1980; member of the International Women's Sports Hall of Fame, 1981.

At those games, two winning African-American sprinters, Tommie Smith and John Carlos, protested against racism in America. They raised their fists in the black power salute during the playing of the American national anthem at the awards ceremony. As a result, they were expelled from the Olympic athletes' village. Wyomia dedicated one of her gold medals to Smith and Carlos, and wore black shorts when receiving her medal. She wanted to show her support for their cause. "What I did was win a track event. What they did lasted a lifetime, and life is bigger than sport."

Following her track career, Wyomia coached talented, young high school athletes and helped found the Women's Sports Foundation. She also served as an official goodwill ambassador to Africa. In 1984, she was given the honor of carrying the Olympic torch at the Los Angeles games. Today, Wyomia continues her work with young people as a naturalist at an outdoor camp in the Los Angeles school district.

Accomplishments

1960s Attended Tennessee State University.

1964-68 Won three Olympic gold medals and one silver medal. Was the first person to win gold medals in the 100-meter race at two Olympics in a row.

1973 Became one of the first professional track-and-field stars when she signed on with the Professional International Track Association.

1980 Elected to the National Track-and-Field Hall of Fame.

Index

1 2 3 4 5 6 7 8 9 0 Printed in Canada 6 5 4 3 2 1 0 9 8 7